CUPCAKES

BY NANCY LAMBERT

PUBLISHING PLC

Published by Top That! Publishing plc
Tide Mill Way, Woodbridge, Suffolk, IP12 1AP, UK
www.topthatpublishing.com
Copyright © 2013 Top That! Publishing plc
All rights reserved.

CONTENTS

INTRODUCTION

The term 'cupcake' was first used in an 1828 cookbook and got its name from the individual pottery cups they were baked in. Since then, the fancy little cakes have enjoyed much-deserved success and have grown even more popular in recent years. From the mouth-watering icing to the fluffy base, a fantastically made cupcake is guaranteed to appeal and bring a smile to anyone's face!

This book will provide you with a selection of cupcake recipes that are perfect for junior chefs to make with the help of an adult. And remember, once you have perfected the recipes, don't be afraid to experiment with the ingredients and toppings to create your own great cupcake treats!

COOKING TIPS!

- Make sure you use the freshest ingredients possible.

- All of the cupcakes in this book feature butter, but margarine works just as well.

- Fill your paper cases so they are about two-thirds full. Don't fill them too high or they will spill over whilst in the oven.

- Cupcakes are best eaten the day they are made, however plain cupcakes can be frozen for up to three months.

- Cupcakes are cooked once a toothpick pricked into the middle of the cake comes out clean.

EQUIPMENT

- To complete the recipes in this book, you will need to use a selection of everyday cooking equipment and utensils, such as mixing bowls, saucepans, a sieve, knives, spoons and forks and a chopping board.

- Of course, you'll need to weigh and measure the ingredients, so you'll need a measuring jug and some kitchen scales too.

- Some of the recipes tell you to use a whisk. Ask an adult to help you use an electric whisk, or you can use a balloon whisk yourself – you'll just have to work extra hard!

- All of the recipes in this book need bun cases and a bun case baking tray. Before starting any recipe, put the cases into the tray and preheat the oven. All other equipment that you may not have to hand are listed at the start of each recipe.

SAFETY & HYGIENE

ADULT SUPERVISION IS REQUIRED FOR ALL RECIPES

- Before starting any cooking always wash your hands.

- Cover any cuts with a plaster.

- Wear an apron to protect your clothes.

- Always make sure that all the equipment you use is clean.

- If you need to use a sharp knife to cut up something hard, ask an adult to help you. Always use a chopping board.

- Remember that trays in the oven and pans on the cooker can get very hot. Always ask an adult to turn on the oven and to get things in and out of the oven for you.

- Always ask an adult for help if you are using anything electrical – like an electric whisk.

- Be careful when heating anything in a pan on top of the cooker. Keep the handle turned to one side to avoid accidentally knocking the pan.

- Keep your pets out of the kitchen while cooking.

GETTING STARTED

MEASURING

Use scales to weigh exactly how much of each ingredient you need or use a measuring jug to measure liquids.

MIXING

Use a spoon, balloon whisk or electric hand whisk to mix the ingredients together.

DIFFERENT IDEAS

Decorate your cupcakes with flavoured or coloured icing, and then add chocolate drops, sweets or sugar strands.

CREATING RECIPES

Once you've made a recipe in this book a few times, think about whether you could make your own version. This way you can start to make up your own recipes. Try to think up names for the things you create!

PLEASE NOTE

The measurements given in this book are approximate. Use the same measurement conversions throughout your recipe (grams or ounces) to maintain the correct ratios. All of the recipes in this book have been created for adults to make with junior chefs and must not be attempted by an unsupervised child.

Read through each recipe to make sure you've got all the ingredients that you need before you start.

VANILLA CUPCAKES

Extra equipment:
• piping bag

Ingredients:
• 225 g (8 oz) self-raising flour
• 80 g (3 oz) butter
• 80 g (3 oz) caster sugar
• 1 egg
• 80–100 ml (3–4 fl.oz) milk

For the topping:
• 200 g (8 oz) icing sugar
• 100 g (4 oz) butter, softened
• 1 teaspoon vanilla extract
• 1 tablespoon milk
• sugar sprinkles

1. Preheat the oven to 180°C / 350°F / gas mark 4.

2. Sift the flour into a bowl, followed by the butter.

3. Use the tips of your fingers to rub the butter and flour together until the mixture becomes crumbly.

4. Add the sugar and mix it in, then stir in the egg. Finally, add enough milk to make the mixture creamy.

5. Put spoonfuls of the mixture into the bun cases. Bake the buns for 10–15 minutes, until they are golden brown, then leave them to cool on a wire rack.

6. Sift the icing sugar into a bowl and then add the butter, vanilla extract and a tablespoon of milk. Mix well. Then place the mixture into a piping bag.

7. Pipe the topping onto the cooked cupcakes and then finish with sugar sprinkles.

TOP TIP!
Serve your cupcakes in saucers for a posh teatime twist!

APPLE & CINNAMON SPICE CUPCAKES

Extra equipment:
• piping bag

Ingredients:
• 190 g (7 oz) plain flour
• 100 g (4 oz) butter, softened
• 125 g (4 ½ oz) caster sugar
• 2 eggs
• ½ teaspoon ground cinnamon
• ½ teaspoon ground allspice
• 2 teaspoons baking powder
• ½ teaspoon bicarbonate of soda
• 235 ml (8 fl.oz) apple sauce

For the topping:
• 200 g (8 oz) icing sugar
• 100 g (4 oz) butter, softened
• a few drops of vanilla extract
• ½ teaspoon ground cinnamon

1 Preheat the oven to 180°C / 350°F / gas mark 4.

2 Sift the flour into a bowl. In another bowl, mix together the butter and sugar until the mixture is creamy.

3 Add in the eggs and beat until smooth. Blend in the cinnamon, allspice, baking powder and bicarbonate of soda.

4 Add the apple sauce and the sifted flour. Stir until just blended together.

5 Use a teaspoon to divide the mixture equally into the bun cases. Bake the cupcakes for 10–15 minutes, until they are golden brown, then leave them to cool on a wire rack.

6 For the topping, sift the icing sugar into a bowl and then mix in the butter, vanilla extract and cinnamon. Add a little milk, if the mixture is too stiff, and then place in a piping bag.

7 Pipe the topping onto the cooled cupcakes and then finish with a light sprinkling of ground cinnamon.

TOP TIP!
Invest in a cake stand so you can show off all of your lovely cupcakes!

STRAWBERRY CUPCAKES

Extra equipment:
- blender
- piping bag
- sieve

Ingredients:
- 100 g (4 oz) self-raising flour
- 1 tablespoon cocoa powder
- 125 g (4 1/2 oz) butter
- 125 g (4 1/2 oz) caster sugar
- 2 large eggs
- 2–3 tablespoons milk

For the topping:
- 200 g (7 oz) strawberries, washed, hulled and chopped
- 100 g (4 oz) butter, softened
- a few drops of vanilla extract
- 450 g (1 lb) icing sugar
- sweets, to decorate
- mint leaves, to decorate

1 Preheat the oven to 180°C / 350°F / gas mark 4.

2 Sift the flour and cocoa powder into a bowl.

3 Put the butter in the bowl. Use the tips of your fingers to rub the butter, flour and cocoa powder together until the mixture becomes crumbly. Alternatively, ask an adult to use an electric whisk.

4 Add the sugar and mix it in, then stir in the eggs.

5 Finally, add the milk to make the mixture creamy.

6 Put spoonfuls of the mixture into the bun cases. Bake the cupcakes for 10–15 minutes, then leave them to cool on a wire rack.

7 For the topping, ask an adult to purée the strawberries in a blender, then sieve to remove any pips. Pour the purée into a bowl, then add the softened butter, vanilla extract and icing sugar. Mix thoroughly.

8 Place into a piping bag and pipe on top of the cooled cupcakes. Finish with sweets and a sprig of mint leaves.

TOP TIP! Why not decorate your cupcakes with fresh strawberries? Make sure you wash them first!

8

GARDEN CUPCAKES

Extra equipment:
• piping bag

Ingredients:
• 3 eggs, beaten
• 150 g (5 oz) butter, softened
• 150 g (5 oz) sugar
• 175 g (6 oz) self-raising flour
• a few drops of vanilla essence
• 2 drops green food colouring

For the topping:
• 150 g (5 oz) butter, softened
• 250 g (9 oz) icing sugar
• a few drops of vanilla essence
• 2 drops green food colouring
• 2 teaspoons hot water
• edible flowers, to decorate

1 Preheat the oven to 190°C / 375°F / gas mark 5.

2 Crack the eggs into a bowl and beat lightly with a fork.

3 Place the butter, sugar, flour (sifted) and vanilla essence into a large bowl. Add the beaten eggs and a couple of drops of green food colouring.

4 Beat until the mixture is light and creamy.

5 Use a teaspoon to transfer equal amounts of the mixture to the bun cases. Bake the cupcakes for 18–20 minutes. Leave them to cool on a wire rack.

6 For the topping, beat together the butter and icing sugar. Once well mixed, add the vanilla essence, food colouring and water. Beat the mixture until smooth and creamy.

7 Swirl over your cupcakes and decorate with edible flowers.

TOP TIP!
If you use real flowers, remember to remove them before eating!

Extra equipment:

- piping bag

Ingredients:
- 125 g (4 ¹/₂ oz) self-raising flour
- 125 g (4 ¹/₂ oz) butter, softened
- 125 g (4 ¹/₂ oz) caster sugar
- 2 large eggs
- a few drops of vanilla extract
- 2–3 tablespoons milk

For the topping:
- 140 g (5 oz) butter
- 280 g (10 oz) icing sugar
- 1–2 tablespoons milk
- a few drops of blue food colouring
- sugar sprinkles

1 Preheat the oven to 180°C / 350°F / gas mark 4.

2 Sift the flour into a bowl, followed by the butter. Use the tips of your fingers to rub the butter and flour together until the mixture becomes crumbly. Alternatively, ask an adult to use an electric whisk.

3 Add the sugar and mix it in, then stir in the eggs. Finally, add the vanilla extract and milk to make the mixture creamy.

4 Put spoonfuls of the mixture into the bun cases. Bake the cupcakes for 10–15 minutes, until they are golden brown, then leave them to cool on a wire rack.

5 For the topping, beat the butter in a large bowl until soft. Add half of the icing sugar and beat until smooth. Add the remaining icing sugar and one tablespoon of milk and beat the mixture until smooth.

6 Stir in the blue food colouring until well combined, then place into a piping bag.

7 Pipe the icing on top of the cupcakes and finish with sugar sprinkles.

TOP TIP!
Make a colourful array of cupcakes! Experiment with different colourings, but remember, only add a few drops!

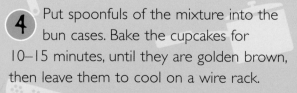

CHOCA MOCHA CUPCAKES

Extra equipment:
• piping bag

Ingredients:
• 200 g (7 oz) caster sugar
• 200 g (7 oz) butter, softened
• 2 teaspoons espresso-strength coffee granules
• 1 tablespoon boiling water
• 4 eggs
• 200 g (7 oz) self-raising flour, sifted

For the topping:
• 100 g (4 oz) butter, softened
• 170 g (6 oz) icing sugar
• 50 g (2 oz) cocoa powder, sifted
• 1–2 tablespoons milk
• chopped nuts, to decorate

1 Preheat the oven to 180°C / 350°F / gas mark 4.

2 Beat together the sugar and butter in a bowl.

3 Next, ask an adult to dissolve the coffee in the boiling water, then beat it into the butter mix.

4 Beat in the eggs, one at a time, then fold in the sifted flour and mix briefly until combined.

5 Put spoonfuls of the mixture into the bun cases. Bake the cupcakes for 20–25 minutes, until they are golden brown, then leave them to cool on a wire rack.

6 For the topping, place the butter in a large bowl and add half of the icing sugar. Beat until smooth.

7 Then, add the remaining icing sugar, cocoa powder and one tablespoon of milk and beat until creamy. Beat in more milk if necessary to loosen the icing.

8 Spoon or pipe the icing onto the top of the cupcakes and sprinkle with chopped nuts to finish.

TOP TIP!
For an extra treat, why not top with two different flavoured icings? Experiment!

CELEBRATION CUPCAKES

TOP TIP!
Add popping candy to the topping for a tongue-tingling twist!

MAKES 12

Ingredients:
- 125 g (4 ¹/₂ oz) self-raising flour
- 125 g (4 ¹/₂ oz) butter, softened
- 125 g (4 ¹/₂ oz) caster sugar
- 2 eggs
- a few drops of vanilla extract
- 2–3 tablespoons milk

For the topping:
- 140 g (5 oz) butter, softened
- 280 g (10 oz) icing sugar
- 1–2 tablespoons milk
- a few drops of yellow food colouring
- sugar sprinkles
- gold or silver sugar balls

1 Preheat the oven to 180°C / 350°F / gas mark 4.

2 Sift the flour into a bowl, followed by the butter. Use the tips of your fingers to rub the butter and flour together until the mixture becomes crumbly. Alternatively, ask an adult to use an electric whisk.

3 Add the sugar and mix it in, then stir in the eggs.

4 Finally, add the vanilla extract and milk to make the mixture creamy.

5 Put spoonfuls of the mixture into the bun cases. Bake the cupcakes for 10–15 minutes, until they are golden brown, then leave them to cool on a wire rack.

6 For the topping, place the softened butter in a large bowl and add half of the icing sugar. Beat until smooth.

7 Add the remaining icing sugar and one tablespoon of milk and beat the mixture until creamy and smooth. Beat in more milk if necessary to loosen the icing mixture.

8 Stir in the yellow food colouring until well combined.

9 Place the icing in a piping bag and pipe on top of the cupcakes. Finish with sugar sprinkles and gold or silver balls – perfect for a celebration!

CHOCOLATE MINT CUPCAKES

Extra equipment:
- piping bag

Ingredients:
- 60 g (2 oz) dark chocolate
- 150 ml (5 fl.oz) water
- 2 eggs
- 150 g (5 oz) brown sugar
- 1/4 teaspoon peppermint essence
- 90 g (4 oz) butter, softened
- 125 g (4 oz) self-raising flour
- 2 tablespoons cocoa powder
- 30 g (1 oz) ground almonds

For the topping:
- 150 g (5 oz) butter, softened
- 250 g (9 oz) icing sugar
- a few drops of peppermint essence
- 2 drops green food colouring
- 2 teaspoons hot water

1 Preheat the oven to 180°C / 350°F / gas mark 4.

2 Place the chocolate and water into a small saucepan. Ask an adult to stir over a low heat until melted and smooth. Set aside.

3 Place the eggs, brown sugar, peppermint essence and softened butter in a large mixing bowl. Beat the ingredients until light and fluffy.

4 Sift in the flour and cocoa powder. Add the ground almonds. Stir well to combine. Add the warm chocolate to the mixture and stir until just combined.

5 Use a teaspoon to transfer equal amounts of the mixture to the bun cases. Bake the cupcakes for about 18–20 minutes. Leave them to cool on a wire rack.

6 For the topping, beat together the butter and icing sugar. Once well mixed, add the peppermint essence, food colouring and hot water. Beat until smooth and creamy.

7 Then, place the topping mixture into a piping bag and swirl over your cupcakes.

TOP TIP! Add 50 g (2 oz) chocolate chips in place of the almonds for a nice variation!

RASPBERRY & WHITE CHOCOLATE CUPCAKES

TOP TIP!
If you can't find any fresh raspberries, buy frozen ones. Just let them defrost before using them for your cupcakes.

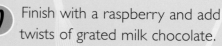

MAKES 12

Extra equipment:
• piping bag

Ingredients:
• 125 g (4 ½ oz) self-raising flour
• 125 g (4 ½ oz) butter, softened
• 125 g (4 ½ oz) caster sugar
• 2 large eggs
• 2–3 tablespoons milk
• 24 raspberries

For the topping:
• 100 g (4 oz) white chocolate
• 150 g (5 oz) butter
• 150 g (5 oz) icing sugar
• 12 raspberries, to decorate
• milk chocolate, grated

1 Preheat the oven to 180°C / 350°F / gas mark 4.

2 Sift the flour into a bowl, followed by the butter. Use the tips of your fingers to rub the butter and flour together until the mixture becomes crumbly. Alternatively, ask an adult to use an electric whisk.

3 Add the sugar and mix it in, then stir in the eggs.

4 Finally, add the milk to make the mixture creamy.

5 Put spoonfuls of the mixture into the bun cases, filling them halfway. Drop two raspberries on top of the mixture and then top with the remaining mixture.

6 Bake the cupcakes for 15–18 minutes, until they are golden brown, then leave them to cool on a wire rack.

7 For the topping, ask an adult to melt the white chocolate, either in a microwave or in a pan. Leave to cool.

8 Next, sift the icing sugar into a bowl, add the butter and beat together. Then add the white chocolate and mix until smooth. Place in a piping bag and pipe onto the top of each cupcake.

9 Finish with a raspberry and add twists of grated milk chocolate.

ORANGE CREAM CUPCAKES

Ingredients:

- 190 g (7 oz) plain flour
- 1/2 teaspoon baking powder
- 100 g (4 oz) butter
- 200 g (7 oz) caster sugar
- 2 eggs
- 1 tablespoon orange juice
- 1/2 tablespoon orange zest
- 170 ml (6 fl.oz) milk

For the topping:

- 100 g (4 oz) cream cheese
- 25 g (1 oz) butter
- 1 teaspoon orange zest
- 1/2 teaspoon vanilla essence
- 120 g (4 1/2 oz) icing sugar
- edible glitter

1 Preheat the oven to 180°C / 350°F / gas mark 4.

2 Sift the flour and baking powder into a bowl and set aside.

3 In another bowl, beat the butter and sugar together, until light and fluffy. Alternatively, ask an adult to use an electric whisk on a medium speed for 2–3 minutes.

4 Add the eggs to the butter and sugar mixture, one at a time, beating well after each one.

5 Now beat in the orange juice and zest. Next, mix in the flour and baking powder and the milk, alternating a little at a time. Stir until just combined.

6 Use a teaspoon to transfer equal amounts of the mixture to the bun cases. Bake the cupcakes for 17–19 minutes. Leave them to cool on a wire rack.

7 For the topping, beat together the cream cheese and butter until light and creamy. Add in the orange zest, vanilla essence and icing sugar, beating until smooth.

8 Swirl over your cupcakes and add a sprinkling of edible glitter.

TOP TIP! Place your cupcakes in an airtight tin to keep them as fresh as possible.

15

EASTER CUPCAKES

Ingredients:

- 125 g (4 ¹/₂ oz) self-raising flour
- 125 g (4 ¹/₂ oz) butter, softened
- 125 g (4 ¹/₂ oz) caster sugar
- 2 large eggs
- 2–3 tablespoons milk

For the topping:

- a few drops of vanilla essence
- 100 g (4 oz) whipped cream
- mini chocolate eggs
- sugar sprinkles

1 Preheat the oven to 180°C / 350°F / gas mark 4.

2 Sift the flour into a bowl, followed by the butter. Use the tips of your fingers to rub the butter and flour together until the mixture becomes crumbly. Alternatively, ask an adult to use an electric whisk.

3 Add the sugar and mix it in, then stir in the eggs. Finally, add the milk to make the mixture creamy.

4 Put spoonfuls of the mixture into the bun cases. Bake the cupcakes for 10–15 minutes, until they are golden brown, then leave them to cool on a wire rack.

5 For the topping, add the vanilla essence to the whipped cream and then swirl over each of the cupcakes.

6 Top each with a mini chocolate egg and sugar sprinkles.

TOP TIP! Change the topping to reflect the season for a year-round treat!

FLOWER PETAL CUPCAKES

Extra equipment:
- piping bag
- rolling pin

Ingredients:
- 125 g (4 ½ oz) self-raising flour
- 125 g (4 ½ oz) butter, softened
- 125 g (4 ½ oz) caster sugar
- 2 eggs
- a few drops of vanilla extract
- 2–3 tablespoons milk

For the topping:
- 140 g (5 oz) butter, softened
- 280 g (10 oz) icing sugar
- 1–2 tablespoons milk
- a few drops of pink food colouring
- ready-to-roll icing
- sweets, to decorate

1 Preheat the oven to 180°C / 350°F / gas mark 4.

2 Sift the flour into a bowl, followed by the butter. Use the tips of your fingers to rub the butter and flour together until the mixture becomes crumbly. Alternatively, ask an adult to use an electric whisk. Add the sugar and mix it in, then stir in the eggs. Finally, add the vanilla extract and milk to make the mixture creamy.

3 Put spoonfuls of the mixture into the bun cases. Bake the cupcakes for 10–15 minutes, until they are golden brown, then leave them to cool on a wire rack.

4 For the topping, place the butter in a large bowl and add half of the icing sugar. Beat until smooth.

5 Add the remaining icing sugar and one tablespoon of milk and beat the mixture until creamy and smooth. Beat in more milk if necessary to loosen the icing. Place in a piping bag and pipe on top of the cupcakes.

6 Next, knead a few drops of food colouring (more or less depending on how pink you would like the petals to be) into a section of the ready-to-roll icing. Once the colour is even, roll out the icing. Ask an adult to cut the icing into petal shapes, using a sharp knife. Run the knife lightly over each petal to add texture. Form the petals together so they make a flower and curl the outside of the petals upwards. Place the petals onto each cupcake and top with a sweet.

TOP TIP!
Make smaller petals and flowers so you can add more than one to each cake!

17

WINTER SNOW CUPCAKES

Extra equipment:
• rolling pin

Ingredients:
• 3 eggs
• 150 g (5 oz) butter, softened
• 150 g (5 oz) sugar
• 175 g (6 oz) self-raising flour, sifted
• a few drops of vanilla essence

For the topping:
• blue food colouring
• ready-to-roll icing

1 Preheat the oven to 180°C / 350°F / gas mark 4.

2 Crack the eggs into a bowl and beat lightly with a fork. Add the beaten eggs to a large bowl containing the butter, sugar, sifted flour and vanilla essence.

3 Beat until the mixture is light and creamy.

4 Use a teaspoon to transfer equal amounts of the mixture to the bun cases. Bake the cupcakes for 18–20 minutes. Leave them to cool on a wire rack.

5 Knead a couple of drops of food colouring into half of the ready-to-roll icing. When the colour is even, roll out the icing and cut out blue snowflake shapes to cover each cupcake.

6 Cut out smaller snowflake shapes from the remaining ready-to-roll icing and place these on top of the blue icing base layer.

TOP TIP!
You could use marzipan instead of icing for the topping!

18

GINGERBREAD CUPCAKES

Extra equipment:
- piping bag

Ingredients:
- 50 g (2 oz) self-raising flour
- 50 g (2 oz) plain flour
- 1/4 teaspoon bicarbonate of soda
- 1 teaspoon ground ginger
- 1/2 teaspoon ground cinnamon
- 1/4 teaspoon ground nutmeg
- 100 g (4 oz) brown sugar
- 1 egg
- 100 g (4 oz) butter, softened
- 2–3 tablespoons milk
- 2 tablespoons golden syrup

For the topping:
- 100 g (4 oz) cream cheese
- 25 g (1 oz) butter
- 1/2 teaspoon vanilla essence
- 120 g (4 1/2 oz) icing sugar
- mini gingerbread men

1 Preheat the oven to 180°C / 350°F / gas mark 4.

2 Sift the flours, bicarbonate of soda, ginger, cinnamon and nutmeg into a large bowl.

3 Add the remaining ingredients. Mix together with a wooden spoon, or alternatively, ask an adult to use an electric whisk.

4 Put spoonfuls of the mixture into the bun cases. Bake the cupcakes for 10–15 minutes, until they are golden brown, then leave them to cool on a wire rack.

5 For the topping, beat together the cream cheese and butter.

6 Add in the vanilla essence and icing sugar, beating until smooth. Place in a piping bag and pipe onto the top of each cupcake.

7 To finish, top with mini gingerbread men.

TOP TIP!
If you have the time, why not make your own gingerbread men!

19

FOOTBALL CUPCAKES

MAKES 12

TOP TIP!
Before decorating your cupcakes, brush the tops lightly with your finger to remove any crumbs.

Extra equipment:
- piping bag with a thin nozzle
- rolling pin
- icing syringe

Ingredients:
- 125 g (4 ½ oz) self-raising flour
- 125 g (4 ½ oz) butter, softened
- 125 g (4 ½ oz) caster sugar
- 2 large eggs
- 2–3 tablespoons milk

For the topping:
- 140 g (5 oz) butter, softened
- 280 g (10 oz) icing sugar
- 1–2 tablespoons milk
- green food colouring
- red food colouring
- ready-to-roll icing

1 Preheat the oven to 180°C / 350°F / gas mark 4.

2 Sift the flour into a bowl, followed by the butter. Use the tips of your fingers to rub the butter and flour together until the mixture becomes crumbly. Add the sugar and mix it in, then stir in the eggs. Finally, add the milk to make the mixture creamy.

3 Put spoonfuls of the mixture into the bun cases. Bake the cupcakes for 10–15 minutes, until they are golden brown, then leave them to cool on a wire rack.

4 For the topping, place the butter in a large bowl and add half of the icing sugar. Beat until smooth. Add the remaining icing sugar and one tablespoon of the milk and beat the mixture until creamy and smooth. Beat in more milk if necessary to loosen the icing. Reserve a quarter of the icing for later and then add a few drops of green food colouring and mix well.

5 Place the mixture into a piping bag with a thin nozzle. Next, pipe the topping onto the cupcakes, swirling and lifting the nozzle upwards to create a grass-like effect.

6 Next, knead red food colouring into the ready-to-roll icing. Roll it out and ask an adult to cut out shirt shapes, using a sharp knife. Place a shirt onto each of the cupcakes. Using an icing syringe, pipe a number onto the top of each shirt with the reserved icing from earlier.

SPRING CUPCAKES

Extra equipment:
- piping bag with a thin nozzle
- rolling pin

Ingredients:
- 125 g (4 ½ oz) self-raising flour
- 125 g (4 ½ oz) butter, softened
- 125 g (4 ½ oz) caster sugar
- 2 large eggs
- 2–3 tablespoons milk

For the topping:
- 140 g (5 oz) butter, softened
- 280 g (10 oz) icing sugar
- 1–2 tablespoons milk
- a few drops of green food colouring
- ready-to-roll icing
- a few drops of yellow food colouring

1 Preheat the oven to 180°C / 350°F / gas mark 4.

2 Sift the flour into a bowl, followed by the butter. Use the tips of your fingers to rub the butter and flour together until the mixture becomes crumbly. Alternatively, ask an adult to use an electric whisk. Add the sugar and mix it in, then stir in the eggs. Finally, add the milk to make the mixture creamy.

3 Put spoonfuls of the mixture into the bun cases. Bake the cupcakes for 10–15 minutes, until they are golden brown, then leave them to cool on a wire rack.

4 For the topping, place the butter in a large bowl and add half of the icing sugar. Beat until smooth.

5 Add the remaining icing sugar and one tablespoon of the milk and beat the mixture until creamy and smooth. Beat in more milk if necessary to loosen the icing. Add the green food colouring and mix well, before placing the mixture into a piping bag with a thin nozzle. Next, pipe the topping onto the cupcakes, lifting the nozzle upwards to create a grass-like effect for each strand.

6 Next, roll the ready-to-roll icing, then ask an adult to cut it into petal shapes, using a sharp knife. Form the petals together so they make a flower and place onto each cupcake.

7 Add yellow food colouring to the remaining icing. Cut into small circles and place on top of the petals to finish.

TOP TIP!
Make different flowers for each cupcake! See page 24 for another idea.

21

COFFEE & WALNUT CUPCAKES

MAKES 12

Extra equipment:
- piping bag

Ingredients:
- 200 g (7 oz) caster sugar
- 200 g (7 oz) butter, softened
- 2 teaspoons espresso-strength coffee granules
- 1 tablespoon boiling water
- 4 eggs
- 200 g (7 oz) self-raising flour, sifted

For the topping:
- 125 g (4 1/2 oz) mascarpone
- 125 g (4 1/2 oz) butter, softened
- 1/4 teaspoon grated lemon zest
- 350 g (12 oz) icing sugar, sifted
- walnut halves, to decorate

1 Preheat the oven to 180°C / 350°F / gas mark 4.

2 Beat together the sugar and butter in a bowl.

3 Next, ask an adult to dissolve the coffee in the boiling water, then beat it into the butter mix.

4 Beat in the eggs, one at a time, then fold in the sifted flour and mix briefly until combined.

5 Put spoonfuls of the mixture into the bun cases. Bake the cupcakes for 20–25 minutes, until they are golden brown, then leave them to cool on a wire rack.

6 For the topping, put the mascarpone, butter and lemon zest into a bowl and beat together. Add the icing sugar, about one-third at a time, working in completely before adding the next batch.

7 Place the topping mixture into a piping bag and swirl onto the top of the cupcakes.

8 Finish each cake with a walnut half.

TOP TIP! Try different nuts, such as pecans, Brazil nuts and almonds.

RASPBERRY CHOCOLATE CUPCAKES

Extra equipment:
• piping bag

Ingredients:
• 50 g (2 oz) dark chocolate
• 120 ml (4 fl.oz) water
• 2 eggs
• 225 g (8 oz) brown sugar
• 100 g (4 oz) butter, softened
• 100 g (4 oz) self-raising flour
• 2 tablespoons cocoa powder
• 50 g (2 oz) ground almonds
• 100 g (4 oz) frozen raspberries

For the topping:
• 150 g (5 oz) butter, softened
• 250 g (9 oz) icing sugar
• a few drops of vanilla essence
• 3 drops pink food colouring
• 2 tablespoons hot water
• chocolate stars, to decorate

1 Preheat the oven to 180°C / 350°F / gas mark 4.

2 Place the dark chocolate and water into a small saucepan. Stir over a low heat until melted and smooth. Set aside to cool.

3 Place the eggs, brown sugar and butter in a large mixing bowl. Beat until just combined.

4 Sift in the self-raising flour and cocoa powder, and add in the ground almonds. Stir well to combine.

5 Add the warm chocolate to the mixture and stir until just combined.

6 Use a teaspoon to transfer equal amounts of the mixture to the bun cases, half filling each case. Place a couple of raspberries in the middle, and then top with the remaining mixture. Bake the cupcakes for about 20–25 minutes. Leave to cool on a wire rack.

7 For the topping, beat together the butter and icing sugar. Once well mixed, add the vanilla essence, food colouring and water. Beat until smooth.

8 Place the topping in a piping bag and swirl over your cupcakes. Decorate with chocolate stars to finish.

TOP TIP!
Top with fresh raspberries for a summertime treat!

DAISY CUPCAKES

TOP TIP! Experiment with different petal shapes. Try to make your favourite flower!

Extra equipment:
- rolling pin

Ingredients:
- 150 g (5 oz) self-raising flour
- 2 tablespoons cocoa powder
- 150 g (5 oz) butter, softened
- 150 g (5 oz) sugar
- 3 eggs
- a few drops of vanilla essence
- 1–2 tablespoons milk

To decorate:
- ready-to-roll icing
- food colouring
- sweets

1 Preheat the oven to 180°C / 350°F / gas mark 4.

2 Sift the flour and cocoa powder into a bowl. Add the butter and use the tips of your fingers to rub the butter, flour and cocoa powder together until the mixture becomes crumbly.

3 Add the sugar and mix it in. Now stir in the eggs. Finally, add a few drops of vanilla essence and the milk to make the mixture creamy. Stir well.

4 Put spoonfuls of the mixture into the bun cases. Bake the cakes for 10–15 minutes, then leave them to cool on a wire rack.

5 To decorate the buns with icing, knead a few drops of food colouring into half of the ready-to-roll icing and roll it out until the colour is evenly spaced.

6 Ask an adult to cut the icing into flower shapes, then place on each cake.

7 Next, do the same to the other half of the icing, this time with a different colour. Ask an adult to cut out smaller petal shapes using a sharp knife. Run a knife along the top of each petal, before placing them over the first layer of icing, gently pressing down.

8 Top with a sweet to finish.

24

LEMON CURD CUPCAKES

Extra equipment:
• piping bag

Ingredients:
• 100 g (4 oz) butter, softened
• 100 g (4 oz) cream cheese
• 2 teaspoons grated lemon rind
• 150 g (5 oz) caster sugar
• 2 eggs
• 50 g (2 oz) plain flour
• 50 g (2 oz) self-raising flour

For the topping:
• 100 g (4 oz) lemon curd
• icing sugar

1 Preheat the oven to 180°C / 350°F / gas mark 4.

2 Place the butter, cream cheese, lemon rind, sugar, and eggs into a large bowl. Beat until the mixture is light and creamy.

3 Sift in the plain flour and self-raising flour. Add them gradually to the mixture and beat until just combined.

4 Use a teaspoon to transfer equal amounts of the mixture to the bun cases. Bake the cupcakes for 20 minutes or until golden brown. Leave them to cool on a wire rack.

5 For the topping, place the lemon curd in a piping bag. Pipe onto the top of each cupcake and then finish with a light sprinkling of icing sugar.

TOP TIP!
These cupcakes taste great even without the topping!

25

CARROT CUPCAKES

Ingredients:

- 125 g (4 $\frac{1}{2}$ oz) wholemeal flour
- 125 g (4 $\frac{1}{2}$ oz) plain flour
- 100 g (4 oz) raisins
- 50 g (2 oz) brown sugar
- 1 teaspoon baking powder
- 225 ml (8 fl.oz) milk
- 100 g (4 oz) shredded carrot
- 2 eggs
- 50 g (2 oz) butter, melted

For the topping:

- 100 g (4 oz) cream cheese
- 25 g (1 oz) butter
- $\frac{1}{2}$ teaspoon vanilla essence
- 120 g (4 $\frac{1}{2}$ oz) icing sugar
- 50 g (2 oz) nuts, chopped (your favourite variety)
- marzipan carrots, to decorate

1 Preheat the oven to 180°C / 350°F / gas mark 4.

2 Sift the wholemeal flour and plain flour into a bowl, along with the raisins, sugar and baking powder. Stir them all together with a wooden spoon until they are well mixed.

3 Put the remaining ingredients in a small bowl and mix together. Then, add to the larger bowl and mix together.

4 Use a teaspoon to divide the mixture equally into the bun cases. Bake the cupcakes for 15 minutes, then leave them in the tray to cool.

5 For the topping, beat together the cream cheese and butter until light and creamy.

6 Add in the vanilla essence and icing sugar, beating until smooth.

7 Swirl over your cupcakes and add a sprinkling of chopped nuts and a marzipan carrot.

TOP TIP!
Experiment with bun cases. Keep an eye out for unusual designs in kitchen accessory and homeware shops.

COCONUT CUPCAKES

Ingredients:
• 225 g (8 oz) self-raising flour
• 75 g (3 oz) butter
• 75 g (3 oz) caster sugar
• 1 egg
• 75–100 ml (2–4 fl.oz) milk

For the topping:
• whipped cream
• pink coconut ice, grated

1 Preheat the oven to 180°C / 350°F / gas mark 4.

2 Sift the flour into a bowl, followed by the butter. Use the tips of your fingers to rub the butter and flour together until the mixture becomes crumbly.

3 Add the sugar and stir in the egg.

4 Finally, add enough milk to make the mixture creamy.

5 Put spoonfuls of the mixture into the bun cases. Bake the cupcakes for 10–15 minutes, then leave them to cool on a wire rack.

6 Decorate them with a generous swirl of freshly whipped cream and cover with grated pink coconut ice.

TOP TIP!
Place a plate underneath each cupcake whilst you sprinkle the coconut ice.

CITRUS CUPCAKES

Extra equipment:
- piping bag

Ingredients:
- 125 g (4 ½ oz) butter
- 150 g (5 oz) caster sugar
- zest and juice of 1 orange
- zest and juice of 1 lemon
- 180 g (6 oz) self-raising flour
- 2 eggs, beaten

For the topping:
- ½ teaspoon orange zest
- ½ teaspoon lemon zest
- ½ teaspoon vanilla essence
- 100 g (4 oz) whipped cream
- crystallised orange segments, to decorate

1. Preheat the oven to 180°C / 350°F / gas mark 4.

2. Put the butter and sugar in a bowl. Beat together with a wooden spoon, or alternatively, ask an adult to use an electric whisk.

3. Next, add the zest of the orange and lemon, and mix in well.

4. Then, sift one third of the flour, along with the eggs and 1½ tablespoons of lemon juice and 1½ tablespoons of orange juice.

5. Mix, then sift another third of flour, then mix, and then sift in the final third.

6. Use a teaspoon to divide the mixture equally into the bun cases. Bake the cupcakes for 15 minutes, then leave them in the tray to cool.

7. For the topping, add the orange and lemon zest and vanilla essence to the whipped cream, beating until smooth.

8. Place in a piping bag and pipe onto the top of each cupcake. Finish each cupcake with a crystallised orange segment.

TOP TIP!
Tuck into these citrus cakes with a big glass of freshly-squeezed orange juice!

CHOCOLATE ORANGE CUPCAKES

Extra equipment:
• piping bag

Ingredients:
• 100 g (4 oz) butter
• 125 g (4 ½ oz) dark chocolate, broken into small squares
• 135 g (5 oz) caster sugar
• 2 eggs, lightly beaten
• 1 tablespoon sour cream
• ¼ teaspoon vanilla extract
• finely grated zest of 1 orange
• 25 g (1 oz) ground almonds
• 100 g (4 oz) self-raising flour
• 1 tablespoon cocoa powder

For the topping:
• 100 g (4 oz) cream cheese
• 25 g (1 oz) butter
• 1 teaspoon orange zest
• ½ teaspoon vanilla essence
• 120 g (4 ½ oz) icing sugar

1 Preheat the oven to 180°C / 350°F / gas mark 4.

2 Put the butter in a small saucepan and ask an adult to stir over a low heat until melted and smooth. Next, remove from the hob and stand for 2 minutes.

3 Add the chocolate and leave to stand for a further 2 minutes. Stir until smooth, then add the sugar and mix in well.

4 Ask an adult to beat in the eggs, a little at a time, making sure everything is well mixed before adding the next.

5 Beat in the sour cream, vanilla extract, orange zest, and ground almonds, then sift in the flour and cocoa powder. Mix until combined.

6 Use a teaspoon to transfer equal amounts of the mixture to the bun cases. Bake the cupcakes for about 15–20 minutes. Leave them to cool on a wire rack.

7 For the topping, beat together the cream cheese and butter. Add in the orange zest, vanilla essence and icing sugar, beating until smooth.

8 Place in a piping bag and pipe onto the top of each cupcake.

TOP TIP!
Finish these fab cupcakes with a sprinkling of orange zest and chopped walnuts.

CHOCOLATE & PEANUT BUTTER CUPCAKES

Extra equipment:
- bun tin and bun cases
- piping bag

Ingredients:
- 225 g (8 oz) light brown sugar
- 50 g (2 oz) butter, softened
- 125 g (4 ½ oz) chocolate spread
- 2 eggs
- a few drops of vanilla extract
- 150 g (5 oz) plain flour
- 75 g (3 oz) cocoa powder
- 2 teaspoons baking powder
- 100 ml (3 fl.oz) milk

For the topping:
- 4 tablespoons butter, softened
- 225 g (8 oz) cream cheese
- 170 g (6 oz) smooth peanut butter
- 350 g (12 oz) icing sugar
- 100 g (4 oz) whipped cream

1 Preheat the oven to 180°C / 350°F / gas mark 4.

2 Beat the light brown sugar and butter together until smooth and then add the chocolate spread and mix together thoroughly.

3 Add the eggs, one at a time, beating well after each addition, and then add the vanilla extract.

4 Sift the flour, cocoa powder and baking powder together and fold into the mixture, along with the milk.

5 Put spoonfuls of the mixture into the bun cases.

6 Bake the cupcakes for 20–25 minutes, then leave them to cool on a wire rack.

7 For the topping, beat the butter, cream cheese, and smooth peanut butter until blended.

8 Add the icing sugar slowly, then add the whipped cream and beat until smooth and creamy.

9 Place the topping into a piping bag and swirl onto each of the cupcakes.

TOP TIP! Sprinkle peanuts on top for a double nut hit!

CHOCOLATE MESS CUPCAKES

Ingredients:
- 100 g (4 oz) self-raising flour
- 1 tablespoon cocoa powder
- 125 g (4 1/2 oz) butter, softened
- 125 g (4 1/2 oz) caster sugar
- 2 large eggs
- 2–3 tablespoons milk
- 50 g (2 oz) chocolate chips

For the topping:
- 200 g (7 oz) dark chocolate
- 25 g (1 oz) butter
- 2 tablespoons double cream
- milk chocolate, grated

1 Preheat the oven to 180°C / 350°F / gas mark 4.

2 Sift the flour and cocoa powder into a bowl.

3 Put the butter in the bowl. Use the tips of your fingers to rub the butter, flour and cocoa powder together until the mixture becomes crumbly. Alternatively, ask an adult to use an electric whisk.

4 Add the sugar and mix it in, then stir in the eggs.

5 Finally, add the milk to make the mixture creamy, followed by the chocolate chips.

6 Put spoonfuls of the mixture into the bun cases. Bake the cupcakes for 10–15 minutes, then leave them to cool on a wire rack.

7 For the topping, ask an adult to help you put some water in a saucepan over a medium heat. Put the chocolate, butter and cream in a heatproof bowl on top, making sure the bowl doesn't touch the water. Melt the ingredients, stirring the mixture with a wooden spoon.

8 Spoon the melted chocolate on top of each cupcake and leave to set. Once cool, top with grated milk chocolate.

TOP TIP!
Don't worry if these cupcakes look messy – that's what they're all about!

INDEX OF RECIPES